better together*

*This book is best read together, grownup and kid.

 akidsco.com

a kids book about

a kids book about

SELF-LOVE

by Brandon Farbstein

A Kids Co.
Editor Emma Wolf
Designer Nakita Simpson
Creative Director Rick DeLucco
Studio Manager Kenya Feldes
Sales Director Melanie Wilkins
Head of Books Jennifer Goldstein
CEO and Founder Jelani Memory

DK
Delhi Technical Team Bimlesh Tiwary Pushpak Tyagi, Rakesh Kumar
Senior Production Editor Jennifer Murray
Senior Production Controller Louise Minihane
Senior Acquisitions Editor Katy Flint
Acquisitions Project Editor Sara Forster
Managing Art Editor Vicky Short
Managing Director, Licensing Mark Searle

First American edition, 2025
Published in the United States by DK Publishing, 1745 Broadway, 20th Floor,
New York, NY 10019

First published in Great Britain in 2025 by
Dorling Kindersley Limited, 20 Vauxhall Bridge Road, London SW1V 2SA
A Penguin Random House Company

The authorised representative in the EEA is
Dorling Kindersley Verlag GmbH. Arnulfstr. 124, 80636 Munich, Germany

A catalog record for this book is available from the Library of Congress.
A CIP catalogue record for this book is available from the British Library.
ISBN: 978-0-2417-4351-5

DK books are available at special discounts when purchased in bulk for sales
promotions, premiums, fund-raising, or education use. For details, contact:
DK Publishing Special Markets, 1745 Broadway, 20th Floor, New York, NY 10019
SpecialSales@dk.com

Printed and bound in China
www.dk.com
akidsco.com

MIX
Paper | Supporting
responsible forestry
FSC™ C018179

This book was made with Forest
Stewardship Council™ certified
paper – one small step in DK's
commitment to a sustainable future.
**Learn more at www.dk.com/uk/
information/sustainability**

For the kids (current and former) who never
quite felt like they fit in or were enough:
this book is for you.

To the bullies in my life:
you led me to discover that empathy and
self-love are the antidotes to negativity.

And to my personal A-team,
whose unwavering love and support carried
me through some of my darkest times:
I am forever grateful for your belief in me,
even when I didn't believe in myself.

Intro
for grownups

We all deserve to be loved. However, as we grow up, we sometimes experience things that can get in the way of accepting love. Imagine the ripple effect that could be created if we taught kids (people of all ages, really) that love comes from within.

As a kid, life presented me with a variety of challenges. It wasn't until I reached my most painful point that I discovered the only way through adversity was to look inward and start believing in myself.

Self-love may sound like a simple concept, but in reality, it isn't something most grownups talk about or have even been taught themselves. In order to love others, we must first accept and love ourselves.

My hope for this book is that it helps both kids and grownups discover that self-love is necessary to create a more loving world.

WHEN YOU LOOK IN THE MIRROR, WHAT DO YOU SEE?

Do you see the things
you like about yourself?

Or do you see all the things
you wish you could change?

THINK ABOUT THAT FOR A MOMENT.

Hi—my name is **BRANDON.**

I have a rare condition called
METATROPIC DYSPLASIA.*

*Metatropic dysplasia is a type of dwarfism.
There are actually hundreds of types of
dwarfism and they're all a little different.

Less than **100 PEOPLE** in the world have this condition.

Having metatropic dysplasia means my bones grow differently.

Even though I am a grownup, I am the size of an 8-year-old kid.

WHEN I USED TO LOOK IN THE MIRROR WHEN I I WAS YOUNGER, I **WOULD SEE...**

someone who was a lot
smaller than my friends.

someone who was ugly because
my legs didn't look "normal."

someone who didn't belong
because he was so different.

I would see someone
I didn't love very much.

Which is why today,
I want to talk to you about
SELF-LOVE.

WHAT
SELF-

IS LOVE?

Have you ever heard of it before?
It's OK if you haven't! We don't
really talk about it much.

SELF-

LEARNING TO LOVE WHO YOU ARE.

BEING COMFORTABLE WITH WHO YOU ARE.

DEVELOPING A SENSE OF GRATITUDE FOR YOURSELF.

LOVE IS...

BEING YOUR OWN BIGGEST CHEERLEADER.

KNOWING YOUR WORTH.

KNOWING YOU HAVE VALUE AND GIFTS NO MATTER WHAT.

It sounds so simple, right?
Shouldn't we all love ourselves
or be happy with who we are?

But it's not that easy. Self-love isn't something we're born with.

IT'S A SKILL.

Something that we need to practice and work on every day.

I know that was true for me.

I didn't have a lot of self-love
when I was younger.

It was something I had to learn, and something I'm still developing each day.

When I was a kid, lots of other kids made fun of me.

People would point, stare, and say mean things.

They would tell me that I looked too different from them

OR THAT I DIDN'T MATTER.

Because people told me that so often, after a while, I started to believe it.

All I could see when I looked in the mirror were the mean things people said about me.

I FELT INVISIBLE.

I WAS UNHAPPY.

I WANTED TO

DISAPPEAR.

I was so upset with myself and upset with the world that it affected how I saw and treated other people.

I was unkind to myself and unkind to others. It seemed nearly impossible to feel hopeful.

One day, I decided I didn't
want to live like that anymore.

With my parents' support, I got help.

Through this process I realized that the biggest person standing in my way was me.

I NEEDED TO GET OUT OF MY OWN WAY.

Once I saw what self-love could do for me,

EVERYTHING STARTED TO CHANGE.

Because in order for the world to change around me,

I NEEDED TO CHANGE WITHIN ME FIRST.

I needed to get past my limited way of thinking about myself, other people, and the world.

That's when I learned that I could

CHOO

THOU

SE
MY
GHTS.

It's true!

In the moments when mean words were thrown at me, I worked hard to believe those comments **WEREN'T TRUE.**

I didn't let them
have power over how
I thought about myself or
THE WORLD AROUND ME.

For me, it means that while my
size might make me different,

I choose to see what is **AWESOME** about me and what my own perspective can offer the world.

I may be **THREE-FOOT-NINE,**
but my mindset is

TEN FEET TALL!

We shouldn't be embarrassed of the things that make us different— those are the things that make us

EXTRAORDINARY!

Having self-love allows you to be happy and true to yourself. When we love ourselves, we are able to love those around us in the most meaningful way possible.

SELF-LOVE....

helps you show up as the best version of yourself.

helps make the world a better place.

helps create a bright light within you that you shine out into the world.

helps you see **YOU** for who you are.

You are the person you spend the most time with, so why not treat yourself like you would your best friend?

BUT, WHAT DOES IT MEAN TO LOVE
MYSELF LIKE I LOVE MY FRIEND?

Well, if your friend came to you and said there was something they didn't like about themselves, like their smile, what would you say?

You probably think they have a great smile—and you would tell them that!

And it's important to see, for yourself, the things that are great about

YOU.

This might all sound wonderful and easy.

BUT YOU MAY BE THINKING,

what if I...

don't get picked for the soccer team?

don't get the part in the school play?

don't get invited to that party?

don't get the grade I wanted?

have a fight with my sister?

don't win the science fair?

feel like I failed?

My answer is:

SO W

HAT?

REMEMBER...

You are not **YOUR GRADES.**

You are not **YOUR PERFORMANCE.**

You are not **WHAT YOU DO.**

You are **WHO YOU ARE.**

YOU MAY ALSO BE THINKING,

but what if someone...

says something hurtful?
hates my hair?
doesn't like the way I dress?
thinks my food smells funny?
makes fun of my beliefs?
says I'm too bossy?
says I'm too loud?
says I'm not good enough?

No matter what we experience or what people say, we can decide to make the voice in our head **LOUDER** than the others.

When I looked in the mirror,
I used to see someone
I didn't love very much.

But now, I see...

someone who is **ENOUGH.**

someone who is **WORTHY.**

someone who is **LIMITLESS.**

I'm still me.
How I look didn't change.

What changed was
my way of thinking
and how I saw myself.

Because of
SELF-LOVE.

So when you look in the mirror,
I hope you see everything
that is awesome about you.

EVERY
THAT MAKES

THING YOU, YOU, YOU!

Outro
for grownups

Awesome job! You've reached the end of the book, but this is only the beginning of your self-love journey. As you just read, self-love is a process that evolves and grows. It's something we need to keep working on and developing in order to become the best versions of ourselves.

Grownups, you are invited to lead the way and show the kids in your life what it means to truly love yourself. Some days are going to be harder than others, but it's important to give yourself grace and to keep moving forward.

Following this outro is a self-love oath, which is meant to be read aloud on a daily basis and keep the conversation going around self-love. It can even become a part of a routine—just as important as brushing teeth!

Every little step counts in making self-love a consistent part of your life!

SELF-LOVE OATH

Instructions: Are you ready to take the self-love oath? Fill your name in the blank below and read these statements aloud to yourself. After you sign it (and with a grownup's help) you can cut this page out of the book (awesome, right?!), and I encourage you to tape it up somewhere in your home where you can see it, read it, and remember it always. Here we go!

I, _____ , vow to be kind to myself and kind to others. I will remember to be grateful to be me. I recognize that there is only one of me, and my uniqueness is my superpower! I promise to be my biggest cheerleader. I will remain proud of who I am. I will remember these simple truths and that I am worthy of being loved by myself:

I am enough.
I am extraordinary.
I am one of a kind.

Signature: _____   Date: _____

NOTES

Made to empower.

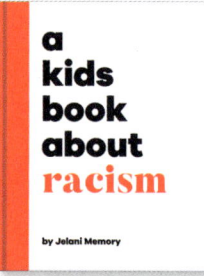

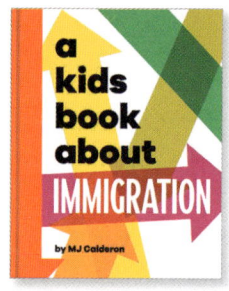

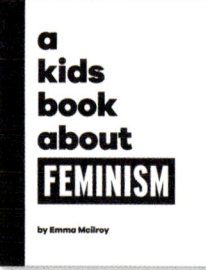
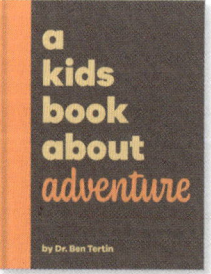

Discover more at akidsco.com